THE SHAPE OF US

THE SHAPE OF US

Clare Crossman

Shoestring Press

Typeset by Nathanael Burgess

Printed by imprintdigital
Upton Pyne, Exeter
www.imprintdigital.net

Published by Shoestring Press
19 Devonshire Avenue, Beeston, Nottingham, NG9 1BS
(0115) 925 1827
www.shoestringpress.co.uk

First published 2010
© Copyright: Clare Crossman
The moral right of the author has been asserted.
ISBN 978 1 907356 07 0

ACKNOWLEDGEMENTS

Thank you to the editors of Scintilla, Dream Catcher, Chapman (Scotland), The Interpreters House, Staple, Horizon Review, Other Poetry, Reactions (University of East Anglia), Quattracento, where some of these poems first appeared.

'Neighbour' was included in the anthology *Piety and Plum Pudding*, 'Fiddle Fish and Wave at Kettles Yard' in *A Room to Live In: A Kettle's Yard Anthology*, Salt Publishing. 'Winnie on the Plage du Sillon' was commended in the Second Light Competition 2007, as was 'The Tile Maker' in Poetry on the Lake (Italy) and 'The Orchard Underground' in the Haddon Library Poetry Competition Cambridge University 2006. 'The Literary Life' was included in 'Going Back' Firewater Press Cambridge. 'Cartography' and 'Sunflowers' are recorded on Fen Song a Ballad of the Fen, (Crossman, Mclaren, Inwood, and Causton).

Thank you to my friends Penni Mclaren Walker, Sue Butler, Anne Graal, Kate Rhodes, Jacob Polley and Christopher Burns. (I am most grateful for all our conversations.)

Also the Madingley Master Class and members of first Tuesday Cambridge.

Cover painting: Oak Tree at Hundon by Rachel Birkett

Shoestring Press also gratefully acknowledges the work and assistance of Kimberly Redway.

"the truant art, the nomad heart. Choose your instrument, asking only: can you play it while walking?"

From Wild Jay Griffiths

For my husband Iain, William and Thomas.

Contents

1.

Portrait of my Father at 60

Everything he loved he collected.
Huge bunches of lilies and carnations
to celebrate gardens. In his rooms you
could visit other worlds of wood sorrel,
buttercups and quaking grass.
His John Piper prints, harsh brush strokes
of paint made dense jungles,
the scent of sand dunes, breathing after rain.

Outside the barn filled up with owls.
In glass cupboards the spines of ancient
books, heavy with the weight of other
readers eyes before paperbacks began.
Blue glass kept the light and held us
in that place, the interior singing
of the world.

His portrait at sixty: thinning hair,
eyes almost grey, eyebrows heavy
with white. The frayed jumper, old
collar of his woollen shirt, behind him
nothing but a wash of green.
We need to remember how to live,
allow the wind and rain.
He returns to me on warm summer evenings,
in cigar smoke, or a glass
of white wine from Provence.

The light we can't pin down,
coming only once to fill our days.

Meeting Edward Thomas on The Icknield Way

I found the track by accident one morning
at the back of the wood. A backbone carved
of stones, a chalk tyre tread making the miles
seem easy. The dog went far ahead, a small
lodestar: everything splintering,
resisting the tightness of frost.

The warmth of another breath was there,
wool shirt, tweed jacket, rucksack,
leather of boots. I thought I might
catch up, but there was no one,
between the black of winter hedges
that closed us in and held the path.

Perhaps it was white light,
an orange sun that lent itself to ghosts,
murmurs of other walkers blessing
the freezing air. But something was given
in the track appearing suddenly and the next day,
finding the book: where he'd noted

each turn and slip of the road. Asking
whoever followed to look again at leaf fall,
bright berries, the shape of hidden places,
marks of stone as he walked east to west,
on a pilgrimage across the chiselled heath,
which promised all the sky.

He must have imprinted air with the weight
of thought, his movement of hands.
Everything seemed so close to how he found it.
In that moment that was falling out of cold,
into spring, which had never been history,
had always been there,

if we had chosen to see it.

*The Icknield Way is an ancient chalk track running from Norfolk across East
Anglia into Oxfordshire.*

In Torchlight

Re-reading them, I am taken back there,
to the first house I remember.
Square rooms, my bedroom window
looking out across the town. Our fingerprints
in dust on banisters to the attic
where the skylight collected water-beads and stars.

The night light burning down,
thick blankets kept winter out.
Under covers with a torch,
sheets starched a warm hollow
for my breathing, and my books
where phrases were like music,
singing a simple world.

I wonder if I seem as wrinkled now
as those relations who arrived
in shiny shoes, with permed
or backcombed hair. Sinewed
and powdered, they looked like
carousel horses from a fairy tale.

It seems recent that I was given
those books: heavy paper gifts
of pattern. Celebration to wonder
at on rainy afternoons. Love encircling
me with what I already half knew,
that I was solitary preferring to
stand outside, watching from a distance.
We never lose what happens when we

are only in the present. Existing in minutes,
seconds, each day a chance to reach for
who we are, those rooms forever
open in my mind, when I knew
no paths beyond the gate,
did not see how dark can extinguish light,
or that I could become so old, so tall.

The Tile Maker

As he walks to work between the leaning houses,
he observes the colour of the early light as it falls
into the narrow street, across the tilting balconies of Triana.

He unlocks the red clay dusted space at the corner
of the square: on the workbench, the solid tiles he fired
last night in cool air, the wind rising from the river.

Today his only concern is blue, the eggshell of plumbago,
the indigo of night, the glimpsed turquoise of islands.
He will paint flamenco to dance under water, tell gypsy legends.

At the bottom of a new fountain basin, they will collect
the orange blossom; shift sunlight to a cold that will restore
with salt and ice the cool of clay, a glimpse of Alhambra's.

Each April, he is asked to repaint the legend of St Ana.
For the saint of seamstresses, he uses ultra marine,
the stain of oceans, the true colour of the Madonna's hem.

On Sundays he returns to his childhood house, the wooden
shutters open on the city, where he learned geometry from
restorers of cathedrals, makers of tin glaze, in black and green.

When others see his work they do not know his name:
Juan Vicente of Seville. A man expert in salvaging angels,
and catching sky to conjure it again in one effortless slip trail.

Neighbour

My friend's mother had a house like this. Draughty
with picture windows, you could feel the weather
even when the doors were closed. Visitors would arrive
unannounced, sit up late at night in the kitchen's coffee
smell or sleep in the attic filled with bags and trunks
among the sands of Spain, where she travelled every year.

The corridor is full of hats and shoes. Vases and jugs,
the deep earth- coloured ochre pots she has made for 30 years.
Bare boards and white walls contain the sun. Each room
a cracked canvas that has caught somewhere remembered.
Whenever I am here I feel an easing, as if nothing
is irrevocable and I could begin again.

I walk out and find her in a large overcoat,
forking compost through seed beds in the garden.
'It's the texture of things that's important', she says.
'Not many really see that'. We exchange books and firewood,
when she's not absent following the light along the coast,
or bashing out clay, refusing to compromise concerning
the details of sunshine and shadow.

Shadow

The dog I rescued sits at the open door,
observing the last of the light.
A lost dog once he prefers to drink rain,
keep watch for strangers, wear only one coat.

His brown eyes see with the gaze of a wolf
who came in, when he found a place to lie down.
Asleep he runs from somewhere he can't explain.
Dog catcher or kennel, he is leaving as fast as he can.

Along the path through the wood,
he rolls and wrestles in the depth of trees,
navigates the mill pond, rising triumphant:
an ancient mariner, whiskers rimed to feathers.

Singular after wandering he returns:
teeth in a grin, expecting forgiveness.
His long pink tongue is pavement rough,
he smells of weed and rivers, occasionally of fish.

I have become part of his pack,
his personal map one black ear tilted
towards the street, listening for messages
on the block, he sniffs for any change of season.

Rooms fill with his harsh fidelity.
His wall eye and whiskers wont let me go
from his following dogness,
his long, defiant stare.

Sunflowers

How he came to love them he is not sure:
deep brown pools of seed, a tiger's eye.

All the words for yellow are never quite enough:
cinnamon, saffron, daffodil does not name them,
too faint and- moon close for their practicality.

Bronze comes closest, forged out of dust and clay,
carved into decades, surviving desert storms.
Or gold a true colour, with its own alchemy to make

the heart of daisies, wasps casings , thick
sugar melt of honey, firecracker, a Catherine wheel.
Their heads as high as his shoulders when he walks the rows.

Their deep amber eyes keep him in acres.
The strangeness of miles of them, *helianthus*,
somewhere shimmering seen from a passing train.

Like a memory of plains where he might have been
a painter, walking barefoot through stubble fields.
Now he's a merchant of the sun,

servant to all those who reach for it.
His harvest horses, the blonde colour of his
children's hair, armfuls for city dwellers so that

summer can take them, across heavy furrows,
into the frames of fields. Their coins in return
for light woven petals:

Picasso-parasol, topaz- ring, straw -matted circle,
canary, butter, parchment, pods.

Home Life

If any one had told her that
it might be of interest,
she never would have started.
Twelve chapters taped along the back,
and a file of photographs.
Her, and Jim, with friends
at the club in Kenya.
Gin, cane furniture, and bracelets,
the other wives wanting to come home.

She sifts her memory,
for fragments of the past.
Those things that make her
who she is at eighty.
It seems they lived in Albert Villas recently,
the schoolroom, the piano,
ferns in the conservatory.
She feels closer to her mother now,
wears by habit, her seed pearls.

When they came back to England
she kept a diary: new ideas for
pasta bakes, how to appliqué a cushion.
Descriptions of neighbors known
only superficially. The realization that
she might always live in a suburban road,
and never be an expert on the basalt stones
she loved along the coast of Ireland.

'It's for my daughter and the children.
All this, of course,
a vanished way of life.'
Home life, a journal of interiors
full of people never really talking.
Her hands move surely across the paper
writing slowly, at the same kitchen table
where she paid the bills and wept.
A woman overlooking a long garden
pushing against silence,
arguing with rain.

Northerners

We have sewn into our pockets a memory
of moors and marsh, cathedrals of space,
crab towns where stone quays push black water
back and the distance is pin cushioned with lights.
Our history a miner's helmet, echo and reply
on mountains, the wild view in the mirror,
warehouses turned to gallery space, Blackpool
in holiday week, iron bridges and brass bands.

Our voices burr with Anglo Saxon vowels
imprinted so long ago they remain embedded,
like diamante studs, hoop earrings, the glamour
of hair dyed blonde, dreadlocks, the jostle
of pubs selling cheap meals for two where
men off night shift blink above pints. Or kindly
as carpenter's wood, railway guards calling
'Goodbye love' when the train is pulling for home.

We know geology and winter gardens, variety
and mosques, chimney smoked yards, rain
that half- moons cobbles, turning them to silver.
The silence you can hear at night outside solitary
farms. Some of our novelists wrote in a tiny hand
in miniature books. Our grandparents worked at
the furnace and the loom spinning steel
and cotton for bread.

When we meet we may talk of hoolies and weather.
Speak the memory of coastal places, so remote they
have forgotten their names. Resorts with rusting
piers where we have been blown inward.
But for twenty pence in the telescope below
the spangled lights, beyond the shipping
lanes there are white horses and new harbours,
a stretching coast, a different view.

Fiddle-fish and Wave at Kettles Yard

Jim Ede founded Kettle's Yard, Cambridge in 1956

They came to him, the man who kept the light,
the tesserae of coasts, the shells and rocks,
the smoothed wood and the stones.
They brought letters printed on cloth,
boats from a children's storybook,
stern lines of winter trees, the holiness of flowers.
It was easy. There was no contradiction between
the waves' arc, fall of clay, marble on a rope
moving like the liquid scales of a fish,
everything had a rhythm and a flight.

He collected sculpture, paintings to settle
on the plain surfaces of his house,
among the smell of cooking, turn of pages,
slate and the creaking of stairs.
Underneath the surface: a basic shape of bone,
outlines of legs and face, arms to reach, cradle or kill,
celebrate and dance, hold up the air.
As well to be émigré, in a pair of worn shoes.

He knew those artists from his journeys,
on trains and planes between east and west.
What better than to open windows, treasure glass,
leave us with a question about stars?

Every day they echo, what he left with cornflowers:
an image of their fragile blue and the sun's blazing.
The essence of what we half already know:
these surfaces of oil, copper scraped to make
the outlines of a cat, glint of horses,
details of wings. Everything sacred to the ground,
and God with many names.

Old Londoners

They walk into the wind, stopping to bend
and examine snowdrops. Having moved
away from the piled high flats with a view
of warehouse backs, where once there were
shipments and now there are guns,

they can't shake off the city. Rely on buses,
the companionship of others, wiping a hole
in the smeared window to see the streets go past,
conversation and smoke with strangers
waiting in the queue.

Sheila's mother's old house was knocked down
and Bill once found a fairground horse
submerged in a disused dock, and did it up.
They still go to Enfield for paints
and wool for Sheila's knitting.

These are the margins that might become home.
Where they can sit by the mill pond to read or
talk to passers by. The pool below the bridge
is a remembered place; pin on the end
of a cotton reel, to catch a dog fish,
see your face in the canal, dive in to make it disappear.

No racket, only hedges. They watch blackbirds
and ringdoves all afternoon:
'Lovely to see them so close up'.
Bill in his cap, Sheila in her one good coat.
Neat and precise as brass safety pins,
two bright golden splashes at the edge
of the wood, among the fugitive sparrows.

Nephews

They arrive in a riot of legs and arms,
thudding down from upstairs rooms,
their private lairs. One is dressed
as Scooby Doo, the other in a tin hat,
for recounting the Second World War.

Silence is not in their lexicon but
for filling with questions and shouts, like
'How is it possible to travel to Mars?'
'Is it true, there's a man in the moon?'
(There are stories of terrible deeds,
 adventures with friends.)

I see one is a sunbeam, the other is dark,
caught in his private universe of matter,
and quarks while his brother sails through
golden light.

If there are dogs, they'll throw sticks
for them. If there are trees, they will
climb. In the park at the ornamental
fountain, they jump across to the island,
testing the strength of spray.

I am given a plastic spaceship with
a mossed rock, and I know I am
ancient as that stone, as long ago as 1962.
So I'm glad they are not mine,
and I don't have to choose between,
elder or younger, science or art. Be fair.
Say the word: 'No', watch as they
grow into very large suits.

They run far ahead, like two six pointed stars,
or small meteors, just landed on earth

Velda's Gift

I keep the etching she gave me on the wall.
Signed 1952, I remember the candlelight
she showed me.

Not allowed to study art, the province of men
with bedroom eyes who would take her
to damp bed-sits or to push a pram alone.
She came home on the milk van in the dawn,
arm in arm with friends, their necklaces
glittering below wild hair.

Her house was a gallery of treasure,
Jewelled bright bowls studded
with china fruit. When everything seemed
possible for her, she was told to do
good works. Her pens set aside like her
bright scarves, at an angle in a jar.

In black and white her initials inked
below a castle where alleyways narrow
and turn, in the dark which must be midnight,
from an empty avenue, a boy with folded
wings stares up towards a girl who is
leaning towards him in falling window light.

I am reminded of how surfaces change and fall
and that in places where mirrors catch the light
to cherish those who inhabit firefly rooms.

Friends and Elegies

1. The Literary Life

i.m. William Scammell 1939 – 2000

Your house below the sandstone farm
was draughty, piled with papers.
Books a currency and poems begun
in firelight, finished by the dawn.
In the spaces in-between,
the garden to dig, an essay to consider.

The literary life, old fashioned and plain speaking.
Manuscripts and hand writing its substance,
oak desk, and moon of lamp, its habit,
for saying what is so. (And you irreverent
and wise cracking, blouson jacket,
an old pair of lace-up shoes)

The day I heard that you were dying
five students played Vivaldi's Winter in the street
to raise money for research. I put some money
in the hat for God, but one magpie flew away
black and white, like an old instinct.

In my room, a patch of smoke where candles
have burned too late. Outside the December
night into which you've gone.
I raise a glass to you, put out this cigarette;
I have folded stone walls and mountains to
my heart, for all the other solitaries

and romancers, those keepers of private dreams.
(that ancient wildness a runic writing
made out of stones)- stronger than
artefacts or the photographs
I never took. More than the rain, so heavy
it's going to wash the sky away.

2. The Other Narrative

For Melanie Withers

There are no moonstones
or crystals in your house
everything is as I remember:
your children's photographs
on the mantelpiece, the long
kitchen table stretching
to French windows
opening on a garden.

You read people, want to understand
what happens, locate places hidden
behind a smile. Plot twists and turns
that make up lives, the other
narratives people carry: how we are left
whole or damaged. The shadows cast,
the grief where knowing stops,
that some survive and others do not.

Along narrow streets, where we bought
crepe de chine, in antique shops
the globe lights, and wedge shoes
we grew up with are emptied out
from 1970's trunks.
But there is still this:
the sea at the bottom of the road,
the time we spend together –
and, after nearly forty years
between logic and dream,

a friendship with its own collective memory,
that there is loss, worlds break.
And something like a philosophy:
that love and spirit come in
many different guises
and are not the only story.

3. Rocks, Stones, Water and the Rowan

For Lorna Graves 1949-2006

In this gallery you will never enter,
your signature enlarged across the wall,
I lift your clay sculptures of animals
and hieroglyphs, feel their good weight again.

I think of your rooms, which were
bare and white, each coloured cup
and plate an essence of the world.
The way you understood the dark
and that we laughed when we talked
about our lovers walking the path
beside the stream at Busk.

Your ships and angels travel on,
your remaining pages turning
prints of wings, carved branches:
recognition, retrospective, beside
photographs of your face.

There was a time before we breathed.
Gone to ground, you have returned
to the fell edge shadows.
We remember until there is
no one left to say that we were here.
I have picked a bunch of alder and ash
to mark a shape, catch once more your grit
and buoyancy of air. The world you
saw with an unclouded eye and filled
with sacred things.

Today, trees are October red,
firing the edge of stone.
Everything insisting on what you
always knew: we are one element
where earth and fire connect to make
us human and rocks, stones, water
and the rowan resist time and shape
us beyond our generation.

At the corner of my eye, a field post
seems to be your grey ghost walking,
toward somewhere full of dancing
I can't yet see.

4. Postcard from Black Mountain

For Simon

There's a black horse on the Black Mountain
outside this room: who lives by water, beside a wood
in a half-timbered barn. Today there are bees, lowering
as they did yesterday above your glass of ginger beer.
The only instrument is the wind and a soft rain,
clear eyed as the small white chapel at Capel-y-ffin,
we drove to visit in the hills. You are not here.
Thirty miles away, you'll be in your rooms, light
honeyed and spinning, as it always must be for you.

But I am still in your valley, a sheltering place where
those with spirit live and some never leave. Going to
each other and saying: 'Aren't the yellow daisies
in this vase lovely, look at all the lettuces planted in rows.'
I think, if we do this for each other, it might be enough.

The Winter Crown

From the small wood, I cut spiked sloes,
purple and hardy, against winter's grain.

I threaded them through the willow ring,
wired on a paper butterfly, woven with gold silk.

I tied on foil stars, for girls with glittering bracelets,
silver pendants dropping from their ears.

Pine and sandalwood for boys
in dinner suits, dignified and tall as trees.

I placed it in the church porch beside the others
who had chosen laurel, lilies to lie on stone.

Ribbons of blue and green for first love,
to keep the memory of the lost, the dead.

Ghosts, among twisted strands of bryony stalk,
as dry as straw, and the red dogwood canes.

The light inside was gold, all the lead lights lit.
Carols rang, for miracles (how a lemon tree flowers in December).

A old man died, bombs blasted lives away,
a child was found in a dark hole.

Those unbroken circles
that catch and hold how we connect.

In the hope of angels passing over
to reach across borders with their wings

where all crowns are barbed with distance.

Gravel Kind

Small hill town at the margins held me in its ways,
with sandstone houses blown together
in defiance of the wind. The clear windows
always staring at the sun. The old
grey priory candlelit in winter.
Land whispering ancient walls,
a weight of habitation.

I walked the fells above the cobbled streets,
until earth and water reached my bones
and I understood my breathing.

High in the valleys, the houses of friends,
wild touchstones of another way of being.
Between the distant light of farms,
river pools where we swam in summer
and wood smoke on the mountains
above the dark of roads at midnight driving home.

Some places reach into us and we return,
so much of us imprinted on the air.
Always in the weather, standing out of the race,
on the borderland among silence
and the stones: we took each day
in our hands, shared the gravel kind.

Gravel Kind: the way border Reivers split their land by picking up handfuls of gravel

2.

Cartography

An old map shows how the field was once hedged
and strips of land planted with orchards
before they grew wild.

Perhaps this accounts for
the feeling of Eden, branches of hazel and elder
left where they fall.

I never see them, the others who come here.
They have bridged the ditch with a plank,
made a fire in the clearing, put a circle of
stones under the chestnut tree.

But I know they have been here: a thread of cotton,
an empty tin on a stick, marks this rough ground.
I wonder if they notice my footsteps,
places where I have lain in the grass.

We share the same knowledge:
the deep of these woods, where no one else visits.
How deer cross in the first light
with an unblinking stare

like us, when the sky is outlined by the ash,
and we pass through, unseen
and the trees hold us there.

Greengages

Every year when they fall, we collect them
to make puddings and jams. Greengages
stolen out of the heat, beloved of peasants.

Piled high in a box when hollyhocks reach
as high as roofs, we preserve them in jars.
Sugared for posterity, heavy as lanterns.

In late November, prising open the lid,
each mouthful holds July in its taste: the walk,
to the orchard, a whispering green of river.

Or being called in late from wandering the roads,
after forgetting in long evening light to white sheets
in a room in a house you have always known:

a mower cutting a swathe; all the windows
open to the air. In the grass scent it seems easy
to harvest what you have, and give the rest away.

Ravilious' Room

After the Attic Bedroom, Brick House, Great Barfield c1932

Up in the roof he has shut the house out,
the sky the next ceiling above a long view.
Everything is of him: plain, neat: brown trunk,
camp bed to lie down on, his brushes and wickets,
spiked cactus in clay pots engraving the air.
Moored there, an old oar from his rowing boat
will take him up river to be alone on black water,
the solitude of Essex furrows, creaking tractors
and geese. The white plaster walls propped against falling,
the life buoy un-thrown hooked high in the beams.
He left this self-portrait, details of landscape
harboured within, pencilled, exact. The grey arctic light,
half edged with sun, to catch the shape of his ghost in the air.

Eileen at Fifty

A woman with a rose behind her ear,
leans beside a open door, which opens
into a crowded room: where Eileen
in a red dress is fifty, shimmering in silk,
silver bangles on her arm. Wine is
poured and there is laughter,
all the windows open to the air.

As if June were enchanting the evening,
and no time had passed. Faces half in shadow,
sepia edged, cannot stop talking.
From outside, we must seem like
an illuminated fresco from the time when
flowers could change the world
and there would be no more war.

Someone is playing a guitar,
stumbling to remember words he
once knew by heart. Notes float
among the smoke of candles,
out along the terrace backs,
becoming river mist.
Later, Lucy sings some jazz,
old friends embrace and go
into the dawn.

If we leave anything behind,
perhaps it will be a sense of finding
things mislaid. Albums of photographs
open on a table, some of the lost
restored to memory.

We fall asleep against each other,
in an emptying yard,
lucky to have been given a clean page.

The Wedding Quilt

for John and Jean

Inside this silk sash of rose, opening wild against
the green, I am sewing the humming birds that flew
outside Port of Spain when you ran there as a boy,
an island King. The fuschia, turquoise and silver
melting into the watered purple moors that sloped
down hills into smoked Manchester streets.

At each corner, there's a mask of leaves, a fan
of ostrich feathers, a pair of silver dancing shoes,
to tap out rhythm, rhyme a place upon an empty
stage. Hold the moment in light to make it
sudden: full of meaning and then gone,
like a hammered moon, or rain falling on a stream.

At the centre are the heavens we all see, the shape
clouds make: dragons, sun, a mackerel, each soul
becoming another blazing star. How lying on the grass
we feel that if we reach, we can touch them.
The sky connects the miles we are apart,
witnesses the oceans where ships count

the constellations to navigate tides,
ignoring borders and crewelwork, forging
their own journey. Vermont girls sewed in hearts
and flowers: so for the traditional here are tulips,
palm leaves hosanna, a wandering foot,
a small dove in a tree!

This carnival, this counterpane, is all we have
of here. Squares of cotton, transformed to tides
of colour, becoming something other than itself.
In my best chain stitch I write these beaded words –
'Be happy'. Hang this from your window, enjoy
this damask, love, sleep and dream.
I have sewn this here, to keep you warm.

Winnie on the Plage du Sillon

She sang to me in French before I knew her face.
In photographs we sit together on a grey beach
wrapped in rugs below the Hotel Angleterre.
I remember how she left her silk embroideries
of peacocks spread out on the chair.

I wonder what she wanted for herself.
An Atlantic facing room where the tide
always sounds. A lover throwing open
windows to the salted light?
Where downstairs amongst
the politeness of all kisses,
she could sing of trees and bridges,
all the ballads of Lorraine.

Maybe she was writing her own story,
the way we sometimes do with children,
telling them what we think we know,
wanting them to be who we will never be.

Too late to ask her now, but
she remains in the ease of other women,
in Jaeger coats, with powdered faces,
holding the hands of small girls as they walk
the promenade, facing January out
in bright hats and shoes.

I know now she was dreaming for me too.
Beyond tall houses stern as nuns
the phrases of her songs return.
Our shadows cast, under the same sun,
some of my look in her eyes
some of her music in me.

The Card you Sent

After The Picnic Party by Jack Vetrianno

That's you in front with an umbrella,
and me behind with a straw picnic basket.
My husband holds an open parasol against
the breeze that is pushing us in the opposite
direction from where we are trying to go.
In our summer dresses, mine with gold spots
and yours with pink, his red-banded straw hat,
and barefoot, we are mirrored on wet sand.

You are balancing yourself with your free hand,
like the girl you still believe you are at forty-three.
And we have set out on this watery day
to reach the cove we imagine at the end of the strand.
Three old friends traversing a beach,
trying to save each other from that
private darkness that turns the tide too quickly for you.

We'll gaze along the shoreline, eat our picnic,
lie in the long grass, listen to the tide, until
everything dissolves to watercolour,
a smoke of ochre, ivory and blue.
It seeming for a moment to be easy
to put the world right and hold it there,
like this painting, on the card you sent.

Close

There is something about those things we don't
have to say. How silences between us fill with speech.

When this happens, it is claimed we may have met before
in another life we dreamt, and don't remember on waking.

Maybe it was the wind's direction the day we were born,
scudding, blowing hard against the panes, trying to come in,

taking the wood smoke and scattering it under the crack
of the moon's constellations, as they shifted to Aquarius.

Perhaps our parents drove the same routes without
meeting, took down the same books and opened them

in windy firelit houses. Or allowed us to
come home in the dusk with mud on our shoes.

Who can know why it is we understand each other,
like blues music and the shadow of ragged woods?

I like to think it's wired, an instinct caught in
the weather of the fields when light falls.

That we start in the middle, know the beginning
and the end, the shape of us imprinted through,

laid down at the core.

The Making of Gardens

for Iain

You are making a garden from this square patch
of earth. All winter you have considered shape
and shadow, how to give perspective to the sun.

You could plant an acre of potatoes but prefer
to sit and gaze at Solomon's seal: those leaning
emerald stems, their heavy ivory heads.

In another life you might have been a naturalist,
all the seeds you collect are rowed and stored
in packets, like the old varieties country people knew.

Now that the sun's come back you burn,
old sticks, chrysanthemum dried heads,
wood and paper, powder to white dust.

The ground gives back what's given:
nothing between you and what you have made.
You scatter poppy seeds to fire the dark.

It will all grow to wilderness, this salvaged wild.
Hearts ease will clump amongst the grass,
toad lilies green and deepen in the damp.

Amongst this privacy of trees, a tenderness
you have shaped with your hands: a long
border, a rowan arch for the honeysuckle's climb.

Everyone needs shelter and a place to dream.
The garden full of violets, or ferns after rain,
floats, suspended.

It's here that we can live, under a few flung stars.

Candle Watching in Donegal

Salt spray and rain have taken
most of the cottage's name,
slaked paint back to wood,
left words half written.

The door wide open to the air,
inside furniture remains as it was left:
unmatching floral chairs, an open cupboard,
porcelain figure of a barefoot girl.

The road to the shore behind is filling
with white bungalows. They watch over,
catching light from the sand.
No need to lock the tiny rooms.
Nothing will be taken.

Next morning two men arrive
from the wake house with a trailer:
'We've come for Mammy's things.
We're leaving the rest to the whins'.
They load the television, clatter up the track.

The place will become sightless soon.
Windows boarded up, no water in the taps,
curtains threadbare with disuse:
swallowed back, to moor and tough grass.
As far west as you can go, everything leans
to the sea. Almost as if it had always been
dreaming of leaving the inhospitable land.

In candlelight there is no shadow,
at the farm where I am staying
no echoes of faces, just white walls
and two ghost seats with empty wooden arms.
The wind blows back from the ocean
across the granite headlands
beyond which it was easier to live.

Childless

Delicate as coral,
you went back to swim with the tide.

You will never have to grow used to your name,
or sit alone to watch the rain, know how love ends,
be bullied by the crowd, or say goodbye;
outgrow your shoes, walk the edge where
the mind dissolves to blue.
There will be no ghost of you in the next generation.

I will never have to watch myself to see,
that I am doing things I said I never would –
your hair too long, the fairground too expensive.
I will not send you to your room, complain of noise,
break promises I made for Sunday afternoons.

I see your shape sometimes in other people's children.
Perhaps they have the colour of your eyes,
the outline of your hands. I wonder if you would
have sung or run. But it is not you.
The distances between us hold no expectation.

You remain a moment of embrace, a manuscript
with just the first stave written. Live in elements
of sand, in rock pools when the sea is out.
You glimmer, racing at the edge of sight.

I sing you lullabies across the dark.

In Yorkshire

I think of it as Emily's rain,
the way it falls on your face,
cold as a spring carrying
the weight of all water.
And the wind drives you inward
toward the fire, to lock doors,
shut the curtains, sit close
to the grate.

We huddle in its bleakness,
shelter in the small chapel
that echoes of preachers
and sermons of damp.
The rain has erased the graveyard
names, filled them with moss,
softened angels and cherubs
almost to skin.

The solitary houses with blackened walls
stare back solid and oak framed.
When it stops we walk out into
the glassy air, upturned leaves
that float lapping at the dead,
taking them back to the elements.

And we are no more than small figures
in a valley stepping out on the granite
road for home. And somewhere
beyond us, the ghost of a woman
in a high house, who saw the savageness
and named it, before wildness took her,
and scattered her and her papers
to the sky.

The Orchard Underground

Plaster walls creak in temperate weather,
bunches of lavender hang from the beams.
Hands have woven reeds to thatch,
turned willows to baskets, shored up grain
against the river, tamed the myth of storms.

At the door of the house, the spirits of cats
watch over: arrivals of friends, departures of children.
Whoever crosses the lintel will be guided
by their acrobatic bones, liquid eyes, black tails
disappearing around stone corners
among a pilgrimage of shoes.

Outside, the garden slopes away
above an orchard underground.
Trees buried in shell- grain, oaks preserved
in marshes where they fell, throw up circles
from roots reaching through fossils
to an inland sea that keeps all the drowned.

Loch keepers and Fen children sail in
caves and green tunnels, fish eyes painted
on their boats, with the ghosts of apple men
and their wives, swimming and fishing
to the world's core.

Not so far to cast a silver net
reach out to touch the grain,
into all the caverns of the earth,
the palaces of trees: and keep them close.
The ash casts a broad shadow.
Flint and chalk shore up the yard,
moths blunder in across a threshold ringed with light.

The Ghosts of Me: *Poems for my Mother (Charmian 1927-2008)*

1. The Ghosts of Me

Strange how I still feel like her,
the girl in the photograph who sits on the lawn.
I still have that dress. It smells of grass and orchards,
if I hold it close enough it takes me to the sea.
Salt stained, it was red as poppies.
We camped in early summer, travelled the empty roads,
met men who romanced us with cheap meals and wine.

My wedding dress is in a suitcase underneath the bed.
I still want to hand it down, the ivory satin,
the net, to someone else wearing pearls,
with a smooth neck and brown hair falling like silk.
Occasionally I find a thread from its dissolving lace.
I was slim as a willow when I first held his hand.

My body has stiffened with the weight of getting
from there to here. The woman I was, the wife I am,
and inside me the child with the pudding basin hair
who is laughing to discover that life is like different
pools, separate and connecting.
We begin and end as bones and skin.

My face in the mirror, my gnarled hands,
this woollen cardigan and thick shoes.
In between reflections, those things I learned:
the smile and furrows around my eyes,
the way that years accumulate and that
it matters how we live.
The clothes in the wardrobe, ghosts of me.

2. Weather Watching

My mother weather watches these days,
no longer goes out alone, and lives on bread.
In the brightness of the sun she can see ice
in gutters and the pavement's treachery.

Feathers she found in the wood below the house
she keeps in a glass pot. The sienna brown
of pheasants' plumes remind her of trees,
paths in the wood below the house.

She dresses neatly every morning, cardigan buttoned
to the neck, before she sits to look out at the street.
The stark red berries, the Christmas roses in the border,
as if she is waiting for the world to begin.

She says she feels stiffness: her legs are wearing out,
refusing to hold her up. At night I see her in the garden
in an old coat, a glimpse of white hair,
walking slowly the hedges that make the boundary, like a nun.

She is talking to my father, telling him how she sold
the house they shared. Almost as if each floorboard creak,
object mislaid, is him concerned for her
in an upstairs room where he rustles the newspaper.

He is with her somewhere waiting.
As it was on December nights when they were glamorous
and he was a visitor from a strange town.
She comes back in, to weather watch again:

above the street lamps and the roofs which hold the sky line
of a northern town where seasons change slowly.
And one light from her room falls, square
onto a patch of grass, on a night of snowfall and stars.

3. The Women

Beyond the morning rush on any ordinary street,
there will be women caring for the old.

They will open curtains, make cups of tea,
lift, wash and settle; keep the kitchen exact.

Among the kitchen steam, they will fill the day
with conversation, inhabit slowness, hear the clock's tick.

These are the quiet rooms: sheets carefully
turned down, hairbrushes kept with combs, pillows

raised to support shoulders, turn faces to the sun.
From photographs and memory the women know

that this was someone, who loved,
met with friends, took buses in the rain.

Do they ever wonder who will care for them
when they sit alone behind ivy-covered walls?

Or will they simply melt back into
the mercy of the air, having understood

how age takes our future and can mark
the present with the openness of children

and the difficulty of leaving all this:
light, warmth, the softness,

the deep shade cast by trees.

4. Echo

Becoming more like her I begin to notice
small things. How dust collects and sheets
wear out, the need for lists. There is
grey in my hair and my hips are thickening.
I hear myself use her phrases, keeping
rubber bands, saving pennies for stamps.

My mother who straightened cushions,
hoovered all the rooms, echoes in me
as I pick up the phone when it rings late,
call 'Be careful' to children when they climb trees.

In summer we picked sweet peas,
ordinary and everlasting. Their paper petal wings
and lipstick colours made it seem easy to
be growing up. We filled bowls with them,
scented rooms with their promise of romance.

These things about her stay with me:
collecting apples in the orchard, visiting
bluebell woods, the adventure of an afternoon in town.
After belonging in the house, a chance
to see our breath; drink in the light and air.

I walk now where her footsteps went
along the corridors into the garden.
The keeping of the seasons always falling to us
and all the details which make a kind of home.

5. The Last House that is Home

Beside the phone, blue petals from the dried
hydrangeas fall, the shadows of the years we
spent together. On the walls two prints of framed
anemone you were given as a wedding present.

You live in silence now, we feed you, lift you,
brush your hair. At the bottom of the kitchen
cupboard, vases and bowls and jugs lie empty
as if one day you will return to fill them to the brim.

But you have gone from us, the woman who
grew irises, wrote letters with a fountain pen.
I fall asleep sometimes and dream that everything
is as it was - we are outside the solid Northern house

in the garden, surrounded by trees and fields,
or cutting mistletoe and holly to decorate,
the hall. The yellow wallpaper still in place,
the shape you gave the rooms.

The years accumulate, they linger
in each chair and lamp, pattern in shafts
of sunlight on the door. I still love these hours,
the chance to sit with you.

It's your voice, when I walk the river
telling me to 'get some air and not waste
the afternoon'. My own hair greying in the mirror,
lines around my eyes, as you sit

beside the rosewood table, waiting
for your mother and father to come home.

6. My Mother's Rings

They are the circles of years of late Friday
afternoons. When we visited the shops,
lumped back bags of jam pot covers,
potatoes, soup, hyacinth bulbs and oranges.
In a ceremony of shelf to car, car to house,
house to kitchen shelf. Its own strange dance,
'a day's work' she called it, clattering cups
after we had carried all home.

Or a small history perhaps, written in
a round hand, of walks across long fields,
thank you letters, sixpences
and red balls for jacks, toffee apples,
bicycles and hoops, petals pressed
between two heavy books, pearl buttons
on the white blouse she gave me when I
was fifteen, for my first date.

I wear them all the time as she did:
When I'm cleaning, cooking, clearing
a space. The silver wedding band
that seems made of cobweb,
then tiny rubies for a girl and sapphires
for a boy. They hold a pool of light,
a hymn of the worlds she gave me:
willow cabins, boxes of delights,
countries beyond the stars.

From time to time, to get rid of soap
and dust, she's rinse them in hot water
until they shone. In them she is still
with me. Everything linked, and not
allowed to tarnish or refuse to catch the sun.

Indian Summer

The Incas named it:

These last days which fill with orange sun.
Summer suspended, late into October,
stamping marigold, bronze, ochre,
earth colours to a bleached desert shore.

Twigs hung with hips and haws glitter in
one last burn. Pink chrysanthemums blaze
with the defiance of a struck match, flaring
the deep scent of ripened quince and pears.

But frost is framing that weather. Dampening
the edge of dark with cold and fog. Moths
fly toward squares of sepia light, bees
becoming amber, all the harvest in.

I think that this is what dying might be like:
a deep tiredness, needing to dissolve but
also being able to walk out, without a coat,
into the richness of earth and sky:

knowing that this is parting, a final ripeness.
The earth sending up a straight spire of smoke,
calling you to come to the dust.
The glass drained golden, to one last spoon.